www.finishinglinepress.com

Air-Breathing Life

poems by

Abigail Warren

Finishing Line Press
Georgetown, Kentucky

Air-Breathing Life

Copyright © 2017 by Abigail Warren
ISBN 978-1-63534-177-5 First Edition
All rights reserved under International and Pan-American Copyright Conventions.
No part of this book may be reproduced in any manner whatsoever without written
permission from the publisher, except in the case of brief quotations embodied in
critical articles and reviews.

ACKNOWLEDGMENTS

Acknowledgements are made to the editors of the following publications,
where some of these poems first appeared:

Chronogram: "A Field Guide to Sparrows." *Clarion*: "Conversation After Her
Death." *Compass Rose*: "The Blue Jay and Dove." *ducts.org*: "Air-breathing
Life." *decomP*: "A Field Guide to Butterflies." *Front Range Review*: "A Field
Guide to Locusts." *Grey Sparrow Press*: "A Field Guide to Sparrows." *Hawai'i
Pacific Review*: "A Dark Night's Lull." *Limestone*: "Summer's Butter & Sugar."
The Scribbler: "When Leeola Was Telling Me the Prime Interest Rate."
Mantis: "Ave Maria." *Tin House Reels*: "A Field Guide to Salmon."

Publisher: Leah Maines
Editor: Christen Kincaid
Cover Art: Scout Cuomo, www.scoutcuomo.com
Author Photo: Kathleen Zeamer
Cover Design: Elizabeth Maines McCleavy

Printed in the USA on acid-free paper.
Order online: www.finishinglinepress.com
         also available on amazon.com

Author inquiries and mail orders:
Finishing Line Press
P. O. Box 1626
Georgetown, Kentucky 40324
U. S. A.

Table of Contents

For Jacob

In memoriam Margaret Columba and Sophia Columba

"Everyone can master a grief but he that has it."
~ Shakespeare

Air-breathing Life

Sleeping beside you
is like sharing the sheets with a fish
reeled up on the boat deck
the hook rooted firm
in your angry, sweet mouth
you twist and twist circles, spirals,
your tail flaps and beats,
slap, slap, slapping
on the wooden planks
I dodge your sharp scaly sides
and wonder are you remembering a time
when salt was your world
and you didn't want change,
but gasped
some strange new element.
I reach my calf around you,
an arm slid in your fin
and wait
while you adjust
to this air, this life
of yours with me.

A Field Guide To Butterflies

The Blue Morpho butterfly does not eat food
but drinks the nectar of rotting fruit;
it lives about 15 days.
I have lived 3 years past the life expectancy of a woman in Haiti.
Put down your newspaper, set aside the book, come with me.
I'll drop pomegranate seeds in your mouth one by one;
and for an hour or so, we'll make death wait,
not concern ourselves with longing and loss.

A Field Guide To Salmon

Remembering the smell of the stream
the salmon returns, sometimes
a thousand miles
to spawn and die in the same place
it once was a fingerling.

The spring thaw and growing light
carries the fingerling
downstream, adjusting to
saltwater, the ocean.

At the mouth of the river
let us set out to live,
attach ourselves to something we love,
fight our way back,
find magnitude in the undoing.

A Field Guide to the House Sparrow

House Sparrows mate for life,
their bond becomes
the keeping of the nest;
so famously sexed
it's said they carried
Aphrodite's chariot.

Uncaged in Brooklyn,
delivered by boat
at 11 months
you too mother, adapted well
in this city of immigrants.

If a nestling chick loses
its mother or father
another sparrow,
hearing the babe's cries,
will bring food.

Now that you are gone
if my begging murmurs are heard
will Hestia come?

A Field Guide To Locusts

I'm watching the locust egg
dropping, burrowing,
14 feet below the ground and waiting
17 years !
I know what it feels like to wait
to dig my way out
look for someone, anyone
to fuck
drop a few eggs myself,
sing
sing so loud that everyone
shuts windows,
just to shut me up.
My wings stretching out of this
crunchy shell.
I wait.

A Dark Night's Lull

The oxygen machine purrs
with its slow methodical
thumping heart beat
the hissing nebulizer takes its turn.

She moves from bed to chair
medication to medication
and sends me to the store
for 50 cents off the tissue paper.

Death waits patiently
pants and takes its own breath
a wild dog in the far off field
just beyond the maples.

Conversation After Her Death

"Margaret, a hat no more belongs
in your hands than
gloves on the top of your head."
So the good Sister
made her sit through Mass
with the gloves
on top of her head.

The only story she told me

that leads me into
her silence, and mine
where we meet to talk.

The Blue Jay and Dove

When Mr. Duffy's drainpipe
puddled rainwater in my mother's yard
the whole neighborhood heard about it,
full volume she was.

So when that blue jay cawed
at my kitchen window
with his royal plumage, arched head
fitting a foul-mouthed king,

I thought about the side of her
people didn't see very often:
how she loved to feed the birds,
feeders everywhere

and insisted
on calling the pigeons
mourning doves
a kinder name she said

and listen to that
sweet sorrow
coming from the backyard.

Summer's Butter & Sugar

I drove down route 9
past Stan's vegetable stand
and Janet was under a tent awning
selling blueberries, raspberries
and corn, your favorite,
the first of the season.
We never have corn on July 4th,
too early,
but the warm spring changed things.
Without thinking,
I almost turned in—
remembering how you love summer corn—
but why buy it when you're away?
Away, not gone, just away.
I drove on.
Thinking of the summer you and Joel
had the corn-eating contest,
you won, hands down,
no salt (maybe a little)
not much butter,
just corn, 6 ears.

La Convivencia

The scribes wrote first in Arabic,
then Hebrew, and Latin, too.
Long lost words made their way
to Europe.
On the streets of Toledo
Muslims, Jews, and Christians
with their lamb stews,
coriander, cumin, saffron and thyme.
The mosque with its mosaic arches,
the temple unadorned,
and the church with its Popes buried
under white marbled floors.
Now empty of gods.

We, too, held
many contradictions,
lives with long histories,
times of blissful sweetness;
yet unable to hold
the swirling atoms of our own
universe.

Once we walked on these cobbled streets
tourists
drinking Spanish wine,
a bowl of olives on the table,
hard cheese, crusty bread.

Outside the train's window
olive trees everywhere
us, running
running for the train.

When Leeola Was Telling Me The Prime Interest Rate

I was wondering if you really want a divorce
when Leeola said there's a penalty for early
closures.
And I thought about that word *closures*
in grief,
in miscommunications.
Making the world predictable again.
Auden said,
about suffering they were never wrong
the old masters,
just as Leeola handed me the pen,
I saw Icarus falling.
The old masters *knew* that
the rest of the town goes on doing their
townie things, and they
still painted pictures of that great fall.

When Leeola said *closure* again—
I thought I might send you a text message:
Is this what you want?
And did I really,
want to hear
your answer?
In a text?
I looked at Leeola's hands,
while she reviewed
my interest options,
her fingers short and plump,
nails painted a soft pink;

and there was her diamond ring
and wedding band,
and I instantly felt my ring finger,
thumb running over
the bones, band gone.
While Leeola
reviewed the documents,

11

pointing at the *full disclosure*
truth in lending,
I imagined
that she'd go home
and make supper for
her husband,
or maybe he likes to cook.

She said what a pleasure
to work with me,
her black eyeliner, thick,
but perfectly drawn across
her eyelids,
and I thought I can't bear to send that text.

And *Truth in lending* seems like a good idea.
I cannot think about the answer.
But wonder how long
I was flapping my arms in that glorious sun
before I noticed, feathers, gone.

Ave Maria

My first year after high school
I worked at Anita's Mexican Food,
and every night,
when I wasn't looking,
or Carlos was screaming
"pick up the chili rellenos
while they're still hot!"
ciiihleee reee aaannnn ooossss
as he repeated my Spanish lesson,
or maybe when I burned my hand
on that dish and stuck it in the ice machine
when Mrs. Tellez wasn't looking,
walking around in her stiletto heels
with every swish of the broom her
hips, great wide mounds of flesh
rear-ending the serving trays swished
swish, clickity-click, swish swish
maybe it was then;
Maria picked up tips from my tables.
Night after night, worse on Saturdays
when everyone was ordering second, third rounds of Dos Equis,
green chili bean dip and chili con queso,
and sometimes one of the Redskin football players would come in
and we were told to give him everything for free, no check!
So he always left a really big tip,
then gone again.
One night, at break time, out back in the parking lot
the moon rising, our escape hatch to somewhere else
as if we could hook an arm through the loop
swing ourselves up, out in a blaze of split moon light
us sitting at the picnic table
next to the dumpster,
eating rice and beans we got for half price,
Maria told me she was from El Salvador;
she pulled two photos from her apron pocket
dos niños at home with their *abuela,*
I miss them, I miss them, *I meees them* she says

to me, or maybe just herself, or maybe to the hatch
she makes the sign of the cross, kisses each photo
and I'm afraid I've witnessed something
I want to bow my head,
genuflect
to something so big
my eyes cannot see.
I gave her a ride home that night,
a cheap hotel with the neon "H" missing in the dark night.
She shared a room with six other Salvadorans,
There they were, lined up in the two beds
all women, head to feet.
Their shiny black hair swirled on yellowed pillow cases
like black rivers snaking down canyons,
their legs outstretched, hard, muscular bones and
Maria said they send their money back home;
Mrs. Tellez knew this, so she didn't pay Maria
the 2 dollars an hour we got.
I looked at Maria's unwashed uniform,
the apron, with a smiling cartoon character of a
waitress carrying steamy food,
Maria's was covered with refried beans and salsa stains,
her hair a rope braided down her back,
tightly woven, I see her fingers moving through each strand,
like hands through a rosary
her brown eyes, so dark, so luminous.
After that night, I just turned my head
when my tips disappeared.
Benedicta tu in mulieribus.

Bicyclist Dies, 18, of River Drive

(for Harry Delmolino,
August 25, 1993-May 22, 2012)

Hey Harry
a bike, painted white,
sits on the corner of Main Street
in front of Florence Savings.
Cars pass by,
the bright artificial
daffodils poke through
its frame—

the article about your accident
is on the front page—
your photo, a sweet grin

but cars pour in and out
of the parking garage,
the bank still opens,
the traffic lights green, yellow, red.

Time, here, has not stopped
for you.
But your mother?
We do not see her,
the villagers
are afraid.

Blessing Of The Letters

Oh, Astronomer
spaceship builder
of the galaxies

look at me

a periwinkle
a snack for seagulls
clinging to this rocky shore
with my hard shell,
and sticky glue holding on.
Silence,
in the salt sprays,
hear my movement,
my rough tongue,
across this Absence.

I could take almost any beating
from Your waves.

Inside soft and fleshy
peering out, sluggish
on the shoals.

Oh botanist of Bird-
of–Paradise and the
short-lived crocus

I search for You.

Abigail Warren lives in Northampton, Massachusetts and teaches at Cambridge College. Her work has appeared, or is forthcoming, in print and on-line, in *Tin House Reels, The Delmarva Review, Pearl, Brink Magazine, Sanskrit, Emerson Review, Hawai'i Pacific Review, The Clarion, Bluestem,* among others. She was a recipient of the Rosemary Thomas Poetry Prize while at Smith College.

CPSIA information can be obtained
at www.ICGtesting.com
Printed in the USA
BVOW03s0034280317
479614BV00001B/7/P